HISTORYHIG

THE OREGON TRAIL:
AMAZING PIONEER STORIES FROM THE GREAT WESTWARD MIGRATION

by Bill Wiemuth

HISTORYHIGHLIGHTS.COM PRESENTS

THE OREGON TRAIL:
Amazing Pioneer Stories
from the Great
Westward Migration

by Bill Wiemuth

Published by
HistoryHighlights.com
Fascinating true stories in less than an hour.
For the curious mind without a lot of time.
— Online Multimedia Presentations —
— eBooks — Paperbacks — Audiobooks —

Visit HistoryHighlights.com
and sample our recent newsletters,
plus receive free books, video presentations,
and updates about new releases.

ACCOLADES

An incredibly important and fascinating saga in our nation's history, told by the master of US history storytelling.
– Trudy Cusack

My husband told me if he had attended a history class in high school given by someone like you, he probably would have gone on to school and become a history teacher.
– Joy Snider

Bill Wiemuth is able to do what so many historians cannot. He can take history and put it in a form that is not only enjoyable but makes you want more.
– David

Bill, your knowledge of the history of our country is second to none and your presentation of the material was entertaining as well as informative.
– Sally and Fred Burner

Bill's ability to entwine the river and history, and a bit of fun, really brought to life each event. The historical background on these issues was both interesting and educational.
– Lon and Kathy Willmann

CONTENTS

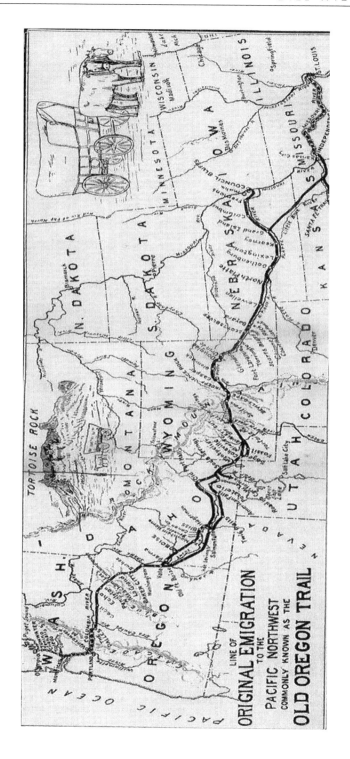

INTRODUCTION

In the mid-1800s author Henry David Thoreau summarized the spirit of the United States when he wrote:

Eastward I go only by force; but westward I go free...
this is the prevailing tendency of my countrymen... I
must walk toward Oregon, and not toward Europe.
And that way the nation is moving, and I may say
that mankind progress from east to west.

Primarily through the middle two decades of the 1800s, it is estimated that more than 300,000 men, women and children crossed the continent, walking more than 2,000 miles toward the hope of a better future. The impact of their migration altered the destiny of the United States and impacted the history of the world.

Many of the Oregon Trail pioneers wrote journals to record their experiences. Throughout this book, I will share their writings to let the pioneers describe their goals, challenges, struggles, tragedies, and victories.

Welcome to this HistoryHighlights.com presentation – for the curious mind without a lot of time, experience fascinating true stories in less than an hour.

My name is Bill Wiemuth and I am excited to share with you this amazing story of the Oregon Trail pioneers. It is most certainly one of the greatest adventure tales in United States history. Researching, writing, and presenting this story during the past two decades has been absolutely fascinating.

If you have a curious mind, but not a lot of time, you have made a perfect decision to join me for this amazing story. If you love fascinating true stories of intriguing people and incredible events that shaped the history of the United States, then you are in the right place.

At HistoryHighlights.com, enjoy FREE learning programs, special discount offers, and updates about our ongoing development of new eBooks, audiobooks, and multimedia programs! Learn more at HistoryHighlights.com.

A love of history grows into a thrilling passion. So, get ready to fall in love with history – again or for the first time. Experience wonder. Revel in these incredible tales of remarkable people and events that shaped – and continue to shape – the United States. Visit HistoryHighlights.com to receive free learning programs, special discount offers, and updates when we publish new eBooks, audiobooks, and online videos.

But before we explore the stories of the Oregon Trail pioneers, let us consider just a few elements of background to clarify what led to this chapter of history. Get ready for a journey of discovery.

BACKGROUND

DOCUMENTING THE COLUMBIA RIVER

In 1792, sailing along the Pacific Northwest coast, American Robert Gray became the first documented trader to enter the mouth of the Columbia River. He successfully navigated his ship over a treacherous sandbar formed by the river's silt and sediment as it collides with the tides of the Pacific Ocean. Grey traveled several miles up the river and traded with the local natives for valuable fur pelts.

Grey literally put the river on the map and named the river after his ship, the *Columbia Rediviva,* meaning "Columbus Reborn." But were questions yet to be answered about the river's journey to the Pacific Ocean. Where did that river originate? What tributary rivers were collected across how vast a drainage basin? How many were navigable and for how far? What resources and challenges awaited through that vast interior?

THE UNITED STATES DOUBLES IN SIZE

Just over a decade later, in 1803, through a remarkable series of events, the United States seized the opportunity to purchase from France the vast Louisiana Territory, including the important Mississippi River port of New

Orleans. The deal doubled the size of the young United States of America and extended its western border to the Rocky Mountains.

Explore more about the international intrigue, secret deals, and military disasters of the incredible Louisiana Purchase story with our eBook and audiobook at HistoryHighlights.com.

EXPLORING THE WEST

In 1803, the U.S. knew little about the vast expanse of North America west of the Mississippi River. The nation's first official, federally funded exploratory party was led by Meriwether Lewis and William Clark.

Their expedition departed from St. Louis in 1804 on an incredible journey across the continent. Their story is one of the great adventure tales in U.S. history. Departing from St. Louis in May of 1804, they traveled upstream against the current of the Missouri River averaging only about 14 miles per day. Reaching the river's headwaters more than a year later, they acquired horses from the Native Americans to carry their cargo over the formidable Rocky Mountains. They carved out new canoes and continued down the Clearwater, Snake, and Columbia Rivers to reach the Pacific Ocean in November 1805.

The following spring the expedition began an equally remarkable return journey where the party split into several divisions to explore even more land. They endured two brutal winters, incredible physical exertion, and met about 50 different tribes of Native Americans. William Clark estimated their round trip from St. Louis to the Pacific Ocean and back at more than 8,000 miles. Their successful return in 1806 spread news of the great opportunities in the West.

Explore the adventure and significance of the fascinating Lewis and Clark Expedition with our History Highlights two-part series of books.

AN ATTEMPT AT EMPIRE

Lewis and Clark recorded an enormous amount of information about the Pacific Northwest. A particular element of their reports proved to have special economic importance: the Northwest was full of fur-bearing animals. That caught the attention of fur trader and business tycoon John Jacob Astor. He had already made a fortune in the profitable fur pelt market. Learning of the great bounty of fur-bearing animals in the West, he organized the Pacific Fur Company to harvest those riches. He sent one group by ship around the tip of South America to the mouth of the Columbia River to rendezvous with a second group sent overland to follow Lewis and Clark's pathway to the Pacific.

Astor's representatives began construction on a fort at the mouth of the Columbia river in the spring of 1811. As the first United States settlement west of the Rocky Mountains, the men named the location Fort Astoria in honor of their patron, John Jacob Astor.

With the outbreak of hostilities with the British during the War of 1812, Fort Astoria was threatened in 1813 by an armed group of British from the North West Company fur trade enterprise. To avoid conflict, the Astorians sold them the fort and its inventory.

To provide Astor with progress updates, a group of the Astorians returned over land across the continent and were introduced by the Native Americans to a low-elevation pass through the Rocky Mountains which they called South Pass. This route had remained unknown to the Lewis and Clark Expedition who crossed the Rocky Mountains much further to the north. This easier shortcut across the continental divide became the preferred route for future travelers. HistoryHighlights.com offers an entire eBook and audiobook spotlighting the incredible efforts and disasters in the tale of the Astorians.

AN UNUSUAL SHARED CLAIM

After the War of 1812, Britain and the U.S. endeavored to mend their conflicts and develop a better trade relationship. So, in 1818, the two countries agreed to share claim to the Pacific Northwest and allow equal access for traders of both countries. This unprecedented agreement was renewed and extended for the next 28 years.

During the U.S. and Britain's cohabitation from the 1820s to the 1840s, the British Hudson's Bay Company fur-trapping enterprise dominated control of the region. They moved their headquarters from the inclement weather at the Columbia River's mouth to a milder inland location near the Columbia's confluence with the Willamette River, as a place they called Fort Vancouver.

Both Spain and Russia also had claimed portions of the region but had released their claims by 1824. The major reason Britain eventually signed away their Oregon Country ownership claims in 1846 was because of the enormous influx of American settlers that emigrated to the Northwest along the Oregon Trail. This is their story.

WHY GO?

EARLY OREGON COUNTRY ADVOCATES

Throughout the early 1800s, citizens of the United States grew increasingly intrigued by the stories of the Pacific Northwest. Only a handful of Americans had visited the region. The exploratory expedition led by Meriwether Lewis and William Clark returned with amazing reports. Meriwether Lewis had praised the Willamette River valley's verdant land and mild climate. He predicted remarkable things for the area when he wrote on March 30, 1806:

This valley would be competent to the maintenance of 40 or 50 thousand souls if properly cultivated and is indeed the only desirable situation for a settlement which I have seen on the west side of the Rocky Mountains.

After reading Lewis and Clark's journals in 1817, Hall Jackson Kelley was inspired about the Oregon Country. He wrote,

...this region must, at no remote period, become of vast importance to our Government, and of deep and general interest... Oregon must, eventually, become a

favorite field of modern enterprise, and the abode of civilization.

Kelley claimed that he then "conceived the plan of its colonization, and the founding of a new republic of civil and religious freedom, on the shores of the Pacific Ocean."

In the early 1830s efforts by entrepreneurs like Hall Jackson Kelley and Nathaniel Wyeth to develop the Oregon Country publicized the opportunities of the region.

Kelly had founded the American Society for Encouraging the Settlement of the Oregon Country. In 1831, the organization submitted an appeal to Congress which included:

...if that country should be settled under the auspices of the Government of the United States of America... great benefits must result to mankind. They believe that there, the skillful and persevering hand of industry might be employed with unparalleled advantage; that there, Science and the Arts, the invaluable privilege of a free and liberal government, and the refinements and ordinances of Christianity, diffusing each its blessing, would harmoniously unite in meliorating the moral condition of the Indians, in promoting the comfort and happiness of the settlers, and in augmenting the wealth and power of the Republic.

The publication's praise continued:

The uniform testimony of an intelligent multitude have established the fact, that the country in question, is the most valuable of all the unoccupied parts of the earth. Its peculiar location and facilities, and physical resources for trade and commerce; its contiguous markets; its salubrity of climate; its fertility of soil; its rich and abundant productions; its extensive forests of valuable timber; and its great water channel diversifying, by its numerous branches the whole country, and spreading canals through every part of it, are sure indications that Providence has designed this last reach of enlightened emigration to be the residence of a people, whose singular advantages will give them unexampled power and prosperity.

As the letters of the Northwest's early explorers, fur-trappers, entrepreneurs, and missionaries were carried back to New England, they were widely published. They praised the region as a land of fertile soil, temperate climate, endless timber, meadows filled with game, and rivers teaming with fish.

In 1840, the St. Louis newspaper *Missouri Republican*, published the lyrics to "The Oregon Song:"

To the far-far off Pacific sea,
Will you go - will you go - dear girl with me?
By a quiet brook, in a lovely spot
We'll jump from our wagon and build our cot!

Then hip-hurrah for the prairie life!
Hip-hurrah for the mountain strife
And if rifles must crack, if we swords must draw,
Our country forever, hurrah, hurrah!

SALVATION AND HOPE

Stories had been shared that four Nez Perce Natives traveled to St. Louis in the early 1830s to ask William Clark to send someone to teach them about Christianity. Within five years, several missions were founded across the Northwest to convert the Native Americans. Pioneer missionaries including Jason Lee, Eliza and Henry Spalding, and Narcissa and Marcus Whitman.

Many Oregon Trail pioneers moved west in hope of a new life and to escape the turmoil of a United States economic collapse that became known as The Panic of 1837. President Andrew Jackson had dismantled the national bank and distributed federal funds among several state banks. Many of those unregulated banks extended massive lending to empower western land speculation. In July of 1836, Jackson issued an Executive Order requiring that government land sale payments be exclusively in gold or silver. This caused a rush on the banks to redeem paper money for gold or silver. The extension of credit dramatically decreased. Banks soon refused to redeem paper money at full face value. About 40 percent of the nation's banks closed. This resulted in one of the most severe depressions in U.S. history which extended for several years. Unemployment soared, repossessions were rampant, and many families lost their farms and homes.

As the Panic of 1837 expanded into desperation, many people began to consider the Pacific Northwest as an opportunity to start anew. Wagon trains to the west grew larger and larger.

Jesse Applegate in 1843 wrote,

Twelve months ago I labored to advance - now I struggle harder to retain my position. This state of things created much discontent and restlessness among a people who had for many generations been nomadic, and had been taught by the example of their ancestors to seek a home in a 'new country' as a sure way of bettering their condition.

James Willis Nesmith in 1843 recorded

I was a poor, homeless youth, destitute alike of friends, money and education. Actuated by a restless spirit of adventure, one place was to me the same as another. No tie of near kindred or possessions bound me to any spot on the earth's surface. Thinking my condition might be made better, and knowing it could not be worse, I took the leap in the dark.

When the Methodist mission board decided to close the Whitman mission in 1842, Marcus Whitman traveled across the continent to Boston to successfully appeal their decision. On his return to the mission in the spring of

1843, he served as a guide for the first large wagon train which included about 1,000 people.

Early wagon trains stopped for assistance at the Whitman's mission near today's Walla Walla, Washington. Narcissa Whitman wrote:

The season has arrived when the emigrants are beginning to pass us on their way to the Willamette. Last season there were such a multitude of starving people passed us, that quite drained us of our provisions, except potatoes. Husband has been endeavoring this summer to cultivate so as to be able to impart without so much distressing ourselves.

Catherine Sager in 1844 recorded:

My father was one of the restless ones who are not content to remain in one place long at a time. In 1843 Doctor Whitman had taken a train of emigrant wagons across the Rocky Mountains. This was the theme of much conversation among the neighbors. ... Father had already become restless, and talked of going to Texas. But mother, hearing much about the healthfulness of Oregon, preferred to go there... It is well that we can not look into the future and see what is before us.

As you can tell, these earlier travelers also often were excellent writers. When possible, we try to feature passages from pioneer diaries to illustrate their incredible journey.

Keturah Belknap in 1848 recorded:

The past winter there has been a strange fever raging here. It is the Oregon Fever. It seems to be contagious and it is raging terribly. Nothing seems to stop it but to tear up and take a six months trip across the plains with ox teams to the Pacific Ocean. Everything was out of place and all was excitement and commotion.

Jesse Quinn Thornton traveled the Oregon Trail in 1846 and described the impact of the United States economic woes when he wrote,

Many...were removing to Oregon with the hope...of obtaining from the government of the United States a grant of land which would enable them to maintain their families in honorable independence. Some had become involved in pecuniary embarrassments, and having sold their property to pay their creditors, could not consent to remain where they must necessarily see their former pleasant homes in other hands. Others had...their yearly acquisitions taken from them by eager creditors who had thus crippled their resources, depressed their energies, and deprived them of all hope of either paying their debts or of being able to educate their children.

But Thornton also recorded that the pioneers were inspired by a variety of motivations. He wrote, "Some were actuated by mere love of change; many more by a spirit of enterprise and adventure; and a few, I believe, knew not exactly why they were thus upon the road."

James Nesmith in 1843 recorded an insightful perspective:

> *Then it may be asked why did such men peril everything, exposing their helpless families to the possibilities of massacre and starvation, braving death - and for what purpose? I am not quite certain that any rational answer will ever be given to that question.*

PATRIOTISM

Apparently, for some travelers, patriotism was also a driving force. Jesse Thornton also alluded to the 1818 agreement between the United States and Britain to share claim to the Oregon Territory. By the time of the first large wagon train in 1843, the treaty had been renewed for 25 years. But entrepreneurial efforts by United States citizens competed with the Hudson's Bay Company fur-trading enterprise, which had grown to dominate the development of the Columbia River valley. Thornton wrote:

> *With these reasons, were more or less mixed up as a very important element, – a desire to occupy the country as a basis of title in the dispute between the government of the United States and that of Great Britain.*

Nineveh Ford in 1843 wrote:

My attention was directed to Oregon by reading Lewis and Clark's journal. The scenery described in that took my fancy; and a desire to see that and to explore the country and return home to North Carolina in 3 years induced me to start. From information from traders and trappers I was confirmed in my intentions… I never heard that the government desired to colonize. It was all a private movement and we came of our own responsibility. We had not any assurance that the Government would assist or protect us in any manner. Fremont Company which fell in after us I understood was employed by the Government.

In 1844, James K. Polk was elected as United States President in great part due to his advocacy that included Texas, California, and the entire Oregon territory be added to the United States. His campaign slogan "Fifty-four forty or fight!" referenced the northern boundary of Oregon at latitude 54 degrees, 40 minutes.

Polk in his inaugural address clearly stated the United States' interest in the Pacific Northwest. He declared:

But eighty years ago our population was confined on the west by the ridge of the Alleghenies. Within that period—within the lifetime, I might say, of some of my hearers—our people, increasing to many millions, have filled the eastern valley of the Mississippi, adventurously ascended the Missouri to its

*headsprings, and are already engaged in establishing
the blessings of self-government in valleys of which
the rivers flow to the Pacific.*

In an editorial published in the July-August 1845 issue
of the Democratic Review, John O'Sullivan wrote, "the
fulfillment of our manifest destiny to overspread the
continent allotted by Providence for the free development
of our yearly multiplying millions." The term "Manifest
Destiny" evolved to reference the controversial United
States expansionist policies of the 1800s.

Polk's stern position faded quickly after his election as
the likelihood of a war with Mexico increased due to the
United States acquisition of Texas. The British Hudson's
Bay Company recognized that the valuable fur-bearing
animals throughout the Columbia River network of
tributaries had been trapped almost to extinction. But the
regions to the north of the Oregon Territory – towards
the Russian America territory of Alaska – still offered
abundant populations of fur animals.

So, Britain offered replacing the shared claim treaty
with a divided claim agreement. The Oregon Treaty
granted the United States sole claim of the portion of the
Oregon Territory south of the 49th parallel of latitude
and gave Britain sole claim of the portion to the north of
the border. Polk quickly agreed and the Senate ratified
the Oregon Treaty on June 15, 1846.

PREPARATIONS

Jesse Applegate, an emigrant of 1843, wrote:

...so great a journey...with no previous preparation, relying only on the fertility of their own invention to devise the means to overcome each danger and difficulty as it arose. They have undertaken to perform with slow-moving oxen a journey of two thousand miles. The way lies over trackless wastes, wide and deep rivers, ragged and lofty mountains...

In the 1840s, the western extent of steamboat travel was up the Missouri River to a place called Independence Landing. Westward travelers gathered there in the early part of the year to prepare for a journey of 2,000 miles that would require more than four months. Emigrants struggled to decide what items they would need to survive the wilderness trek and to start a new life in the Northwest. Then they also had to evaluate how to transport those goods and supplies.

Emigrant Peter Burnett in 1844 made these recommendations:

The loading should consist mostly of provisions. Emigrants should not burden themselves with furniture, or many beds; and a few light trunks, or very light boxes, might be brought to pack clothes in...All heavy articles should be left...Clothes enough to last a year, and several pair of strong, heavy shoes to each person...

In 1847, Joel Palmer published a guide for Oregon Trail travelers and recommended for each adult:

two hundred pounds of flour, thirty pounds of pilot bread, seventy-five pounds of bacon, ten pound of rice, five pounds of coffee, two pounds of tea, twenty-five pounds of sugar, half a bushel of dried beans, one bushel of dried fruit, two pound of saleratus [baking soda], ten pounds of salt, half a bushel of corn meal; and it is well to have half a bushel of corn, parched and ground; a small keg of vinegar should also be taken.

Many young children also kept diaries. Sarah Bird Sprenger was age 10 when her family made the journey in 1852. She wrote,

All winter was spent getting ready for the trip. Father sold his woolen factory and grist mill. He and Mother shipped some of our bedding and clothing around the Horn and loaded the rest of what we were to take with us in the wagons. One of the three large wagons was made like an omnibus, with a door and steps at the back and seats along the side. This was where we were to sit by day. At night extra boards could make it into a bed for Mother and Father and the younger children... When we arrived at St. Joe,

Missouri... we remained six weeks until we were equipped with everything we would need, including horses, cows, and oxen. Our wagons, made in Ohio, had been shipped to St. Joe, and we filled them with bedding, tents, and groceries. There were barrels of sugar, molasses, vinegar, flour, and meats...
Sometime in May our preparations were completed.

Oregon Trail pioneers spent about $800 to $1,200 to acquire the items they needed for the journey. Many raised this money by selling their property and possessions. Along the journey and in Oregon, supplies were scarce and expensive. Julius Merrill in 1864 wrote,

Our miserable teams had nothing but water for dinner and we had crackers and milk. At this ranch, beef, potatoes, and squashes were for sale at the following outrageous prices... beef, 25 cents per lb., potatoes, 50 cents per lb., squashes, 2 dollars each and small at that... they intend to swindle and starve us emigrants. But we will not buy from them. We will keep our money straight and live on bacon yet awhile.

TRANSPORTATION

Thoughtful consideration had to be given to the method of transporting their possessions and supplies. Peter Burnett wrote, "Having your wagons well prepared, they are as secure almost as a house...Beware of heavy wagons, as they break down your teams for no purpose, and you will not need them..."

The large "Conestoga" wagons were just too heavy for the elevation climb up toward the Rocky Mountains. Smaller wagons quickly developed which became known as "Prairie Schooners" for their resemblance to ships sailing across the plains. Oxen or mules were harnessed for propulsion. Peter Burnett continued:

The ox is a most noble animal, patient, thrifty, durable, gentle and does not run off. Those who come to this country will be in love with their oxen. The ox will plunge through mud, swim over streams, dive into thickets and he will eat almost anything.

S.M. Gilmore in 1843 recorded this advice,

Your wagons should be light, yet substantial and strong, and a plenty of good oxen. ... Have your wagon beds made in such a manner that they can be used for boats; you will find them of great service in crossing streams. ...have your wagons well covered, so that they will not leak, or your provisions and clothes will spoil... Though I wrote...that mule teams were preferable ... after seeing them thoroughly tried I have become convinced that oxen are more preferable - they are the least trouble and stand traveling much the best - are worth a great deal more when [in Oregon].

ACROSS THE PLAINS

By early spring, travelers prepared to embark upon their epic journey. The wagons were loaded with the carefully selected supplies. The mules or oxen were harnessed to the wagons. Large groups traveled together for companionship, cooperation, and safety. From Independence, Missouri, the wagon trains departed early each spring in order to make it across the Rocky Mountains before the snow began to cover the trail. The wagons were loaded with cargos, so the travelers walked beside their wagons for about 2,000 miles. They averaged about 15 miles each day for more than four months. Most knew they would never return from the west.

Martha G. Masterson wrote:

Lovers, sweethearts, and associates were all left behind... The saddest parting of all was when my mother took leave of her aged and sorrowing mother, knowing full well that they would never meet again on earth.

Catherine Sager in 1844 recorded:

We set out on our long and perilous journey across the plains. Many friends came that far to see the emigrants start on their long journey, and there was much sadness at the parting. We children wept for fear of the mighty waters that came rushing down and seemed as though it would swallow them up. It was a sad company that crossed the Missouri River that spring day.

Sallie Hester in 1849 wrote:

The last hours were spent in bidding goodbye to old friends. My mother is heartbroken over this separation of relatives and friends. Giving up old associations for what? Good health, perhaps. The last goodbye has been said - the last glimpse of our old home on the hill, and wave a hand at the old Academy, with a goodbye to kind teachers and schoolmates, and we are off.

Margaret Ann Alsip Frink in 1850 recorded:

I believe we were all ready to start on the morning of the 27th of March. On the evening before, the whole family, including my mother, were gathered together in the parlor, looking as if we were all going to our graves the next morning, instead of our starting on a trip of pleasure, as we had drawn the picture in our imagination. There we sat in such gloom that I could not endure it any longer, and I arose and announced that we would retire for the night, and that we would not start to-morrow morning, nor until everybody could feel more cheerful. I could not bear to start with so many gloomy faces to think of. So we all retired, but I think no one slept very much that night.

Lodisa Frizzel recorded in 1852:

Who does not recollect their first night when started on a long journey. The well known voices of our friends still ringing in our ears. The parting kiss still warm upon our lips and the last separating word 'farewell!' sinks deeply into the heart.

The spring of 1852 ushered in so many preparations, great work of all kinds. I remember relations coming to help sew, of tearful partings, little gifts of remembrances exchanged, the sale of the farm, the buying and breaking in of unruly oxen, the loud voices of the men, and the general confusion.

Eleven-year old Harriet Louise Scott described the early portion of the journey, "The first of April came – 1852. The long line of covered wagons, so clean and white, but oh so battered, torn and dirty afterward. We stopped at St, Joseph, Missouri, to get more provisions."

Departing from a Missouri town called Independence seemed significant. John Shively in 1846 wrote, "When you start over these wide plains, let no one leave dependent on his best friend for any thing, for if you do, you will certainly have a blow-out before you get far."

Margaret Ann Alsip Frink in 1850 wrote:

The wagon was packed and we were all ready to start on the twenty-seventh day of March. The wagon was designed expressly for the trip, it being built light, with everything planned for convenience. It was so arranged that when closed up, it could be used as our bedroom. The bottom was divided off into little compartments or cupboards. After putting in our provisions, and other baggage, a floor was constructed over all, on which our mattress was laid. We had an India-rubber mattress that could be filled with either air or water, making a very comfortable bed. During the day we could empty the air out, so that it took up but little room.

Harriet Scott wrote about her 1852 trek, "On and on we journeyed - averaging 15 miles a day over cactus, sagebrush, hot sand. Everybody's shoes gave out and we bartered with Indians for moccasins."

Catherine Scott in 1852 recorded:

Memory paints a picture of moving wagons, of whips flourished with many a resounding snap, of men walking beside them with a forced show of indifference, though now and then the back of a brawny hand was drawn hurriedly over the eyes; of silently weeping women and sobbing children, and of an aged grandfather standing at his gate as the wagons filed past. "Good-bye, good-bye!" say us

children with flushed, tear-stained faces, grouped at
the openings in the wagon covers.

The pioneers found that traveling across the western plains of Missouri in the spring could be lovely. Elizabeth Keegan in 1852 wrote:

The first part of the route is beautiful and the scenery
surpassing anything of the kind I have ever seen.
Large rolling prairies stretching as far as your eye
can carry you. The grass so green and flowers of
every description.

Waiting ahead of the pioneers was an array of challenges including terrain, weather, dangers, and inconveniences. But one of the worst discomforts quickly became apparent due to the rolling parade of hundreds of wagons. Here is Elizabeth Dixon Smith's 1847 description:

You in the states know nothing about dust. It will fly
so that you can hardly see the horns of your oxen. It
often seems that the cattle must die for want of a
breath. And then in our wagons, such a spectacle!
Beds, clothes and children completely covered.

The trail proceeded toward Fort Kearny in today's Nebraska. By 1848, the United States military built a few rough buildings as a post to protect the Oregon Trail emigrants. Pioneers could purchase basic provisions and most took advantage of the last mail service to carry back to your relatives a final message before you disappeared out across the vastness of the continent.

Following the North Platte River, John Ball wrote about the vast herds of buffalo they encountered:

> At times we would not see a buffalo for a day or two, and then in countless numbers. One day we noticed them grazing on the opposite side of the river on the wide bottoms and the side bluffs beyond like a herd of cattle in a pasture, up and down the country on that side as far as we could see, and continued the same during our twenty-five miles' march and no end to them ahead, probably 10,000 seen in that one day.

Moving westward across Nebraska in the springtime often brought struggles against the weather. Francis Parkman wrote in 1847:

> ...the distant mountains frowned more gloomily, there was a low muttering of thunder, and dense black masses of cloud rose heavily behind the broken peaks. ...soon the thick blackness overspread the whole sky, and the desert around us was wrapped in deep gloom... The storm broke. It came upon us with a zigzag blinding flash, with a terrific crash of thunder, and with a hurricane that howled over the prairie, dashing floods of water against us.

Moving into western Nebraska the terrain become more hilly with occasional dramatic rock formations.

Places like Courthouse Rock and Chimney Rock were named for the structures they resembled. John Ball wrote:

> *We saw a whole day's march ahead on the plain, what looked a big castle, or small mountain. But on nearing it, we saw that it was a big tower of sandstone far detached like an island, from the bluffs back, which had now all become of that kind of rock, high and perpendicular, and strangely worn into many fantastic shapes. The detached mass first seen is called the Chimney Rock a striking, landmark in this prairie sea. The upper, perhaps 100 feet of naked rock and the lower 50 a spreading pedestal, well grassed over.*

Elisha Perkins wrote, "No conception can be formed of the magnitude of this grand work of nature 'til you stand at its base and look up. If a man does not feel like an insect, then I don't know when he should."

Thomas Eastin beautifully expressed his amazement as he wrote, "How can I describe the scene that now bursts upon us? Tower, bastion, dome and battlement vie in all their majesty before us... A more beautiful and majestic scene cannot be conceived."

As the elevation increased toward the Rocky Mountains, the oxen grew weary of the heavy wagons. Many items that had seemed necessary early in the journey were discarded through this area. Joseph Goldsborough Bruff wrote in his 1849 diary:

*In this extensive bottom are the vestiges of camps —
clothes, boots, shoes, hats, lead, iron, tin-ware,
trucks, meat, wheels, axles, wagon beds, mining
tools, etc. A few hundred yards from my camp I saw
an object, which reaching, proved to be a very
handsome and new Gothic bookcase! It was soon
dismembered to boil our coffee kettles.*

Father Pierre DeSmet recorded:

*The numerous shattered fragments of the vehicles,
provision, tools, etc., intended to be taken across
these wild plains, tell us another tale of reckless
boldness with which many entered up this hazardous
enterprise.*

In later years, some enterprising entrepreneurs
followed the spring wagon train departure with empty
wagons. Moving west, the had their pick of headboards,
armoires, and large equipment. They loaded abandoned
treasures and transported them back to St. Louis for sale
or to the next wave of immigrants preparing to depart the
following spring again along the Oregon Trail.

TOWARD THE ROCKY MOUNTAINS

After crossing the South Platte River, the trail followed the North Platte River. The traveler's next targeted destination was Fort Laramie at the junction of the Laramie River and the North Platte River in what today is Wyoming. This was the first bit of civilization after about six weeks of wilderness travel. Fort Laramie was built by fur trapper William Sublette in 1834. It grew as a fur-trading post until the U.S. Army purchased it in 1848 to protect and assist the traveling pioneers.

Colonel William Thompson wrote:

At Fort Laramie we crossed the Platte River by fording. The stream, as I remember it, was near a mile wide, but not waist deep. Thirty and forty oxen were hitched to one wagon, to affect the crossing. But woe to the hapless team that stalled in the treacherous quicksands.

The group followed nearby rivers to provide drinking water and good grazing for their animals. But the portions of the journey that required crossing a river were dangerous. Martha Hill Gillette, wrote in 1853:

In crossing, great care must be taken in the selection of a place, and if possible, to cross where there were shoal, for there the river would be wider, but not so deep... To get our things across, every wagon had to be taken apart, and all the things unpacked and repacked, but through it all I heard no word of grumbling.

At most crossings, travelers proceeded across on their own. But, as the years proceeded, entrepreneurs began to establish ferry services across the larger rivers in exchange for a toll. That did not necessarily eliminate the risk. Emigrant John B. Hill recorded, "The ferryman allowed too many passengers to get in the boat, and the water came within two inches of the gunwale... I thought the boat would be swamped instantly and drowned the last one of us."

Moving west across today's Wyoming, the travelers passed large sandstone rock formations. One became known as Independence Rock since reaching there by July 4 meant you were on schedule to get through the Rocky Mountains before significant snowfall.

On July 4, 1851, Elizabeth Wood recorded:

We have been traveling among the hills and the monotony has been relieved by the ever varying beauty of the scenery and the pleasantness of the weather. Today we traveled till noon, and then stopped to get a fourth of July dinner and to celebrate our nation's birthday. While making the preparation,

*and ...contrasting my situation with what it was this
day last year, a storm arose, blew over all the tents
but two, capsized our stove with it delicious viands,
set one wagon on fire, and for a while produced not a
little confusion in the camp. No serious injury,
however, was done.*

At Independence Rock and nearby Register Cliff, the
soft sandstone proved an irresistible opportunity to
physically mark their progress. Hundreds of names
remain etched in the stone.

John Fremont wrote:

*...encamped one mile below Rock Independence. This
is an isolated rock, about six hundred and fifty yards
long, and forty in height. Everywhere... where the
surface is sufficiently smooth...the rock is inscribed
with the names of travelers. Many a name famous in
the history of this country, and some well known to
science, are to be found mixed among those of the
traders and travelers...*

Those inscriptions remain as haunting reminders of
those brave travelers of all ages – grandparents, parents,
and children. Jesse Applegate was only seven years old
when he made the journey with his family. We feel his
exhaustion in this passage he later recorded:

*I was looking far away in the direction we were
traveling, across a dreary sage plain, to all
appearances extending to the end of the earth, and I*

got to wondering where we were trying to get to, and asked the question, when someone said, "To Oregon."

At age six, Esther Packwood traveled west with her family in 1844. She later wrote, "I do remember the beautiful scenery. We could see antelope, deer, rabbits, sage-hens, and coyotes."

Children along the Oregon Trail grew up fast. Martha Ann Morrison was 13 years old along the trail. She wrote:

...mothers had the families directly in their hands and were with them all the time. Especially during sickness... I remember one girl in particularly about my own age that died and was buried on the road. Her mother had a great deal of trouble and suffering. Mothers on the trail had to undergo more trial and suffering than anybody else.

Women's family roles were greatly expanded and their responsibilities dramatically changed. Helen M. Carpenter recorded,

In respect to women's work, the days are all the same, except when we stop... then there is washing to be done and light bread to make and all kinds of odd jobs. Some women have very little help about the camp, being obliged to get the wood and water... make camp fires, unpack at night and pack up in the morning... I am lucky in having a Yankee husband and so am well waited on.

Esther M. Lockhart wrote,

> ...*I prepared to do some of my family laundry work. My husband...carried water... filled the washboiler and placed it over the open fire for me. Mrs. Norton was a deeply interested spectator... and enviously remarked, "The Yankee men are so good to their wives. They help 'em so much."*

Finally, the travelers neared their continental divide crossing. At a dramatic site known as Devil's Gate, the Sweetwater River has eroded dramatically though the sandstone rock. The narrow gap is 400 feet wide at the top, but only 30 feet wide at the bottom where the wagon train would snake through.

The narrow Devil's Gate offered access to a wide, low-level crossing of the Continental Divide known as South Pass. Emigrant Lorenzo Sawyer described the area,

> *Most emigrants have a very erroneous idea of South Pass... They suppose it to be a narrow defile in the Rocky Mountains walled by perpendicular rocks hundreds of feet high. The fact is the pass is a valley some 20 miles wide.*

In 1812, a group of men from John Jacob Astor's fur-trading expedition on the Columbia River returned eastward overland to carry reports to Astor in New York. Along the way, they learned from Native Americans about a more southerly, low-elevation passage through the Rocky Mountains. This broad wide valley crosses the continental divide at an elevation of only about 7,550 feet and offers a terrain accessible to wagons. This South Pass became the primary route for Oregon Trail migration.

John Ball wrote:

Here we were at the celebrated South Pass of the Rocky Mountains...It has its name from Lewis and Clark and other early travelers always keeping on the main Missouri which led them to a crossing far north and more difficult. In two or three hours from our leaving this headwater of the Sweet Water that flows eastward to the Mississippi and to the Gulf of Mexico, we struck a small stream, a branch of the Colorado that falls into the Gulf of California. And here we were traveling over as level a prairie as I have ever seen...but stretching off to the northwest we looked out on the towering snow-clad Wind River Mountains; the very crest of the Rocky Mountain range. For on the north of this, rise all the higher main branches of the Missouri; and on the west, branches of the Columbia river; and on the south, these waters of the Green and Colorado rivers.

LIFE ON THE TRAIL

"Advice on the Prairie" by William Tylee Ranney, 1853, courtesy of Wikimedia Commons.

The Oregon Trail had many variations along the Platte, North Platte, Snake, and Columbia rivers. With several hundred people and thousands of livestock, travelers had to spread out to find water, campsites, firewood, and grass for grazing.

Sallie Hester was only 14 years old during her journey west. She wrote:

*When we camp at night, we form a corral with our
wagons and pitch our tents on the outside, and
inside of this corral we drive our cattle, with guards
stationed on the outside of tents...We live on bacon,
ham, rice, dried fruits, molasses, packed butter,
bread, coffee, tea and milk as we have our own cows.*

As the camp was established each evening, the weary
travelers craved that meal. But sometimes, they had to be
creative to find fuel for a fire and one unique fuel source
came from the buffalo. Joseph Goldsborough Bruff
explained,

*It is the duty of the cooks on arriving at a camping
place to collect chips for cooking. It would amuse
friends back home to see them make a grand rush for
the largest and driest chips. The chips burn well
when dry, but if damp or wet are smoky and almost
fireproof.*

Dried buffalo-dung fires must have provided a very
aromatic campfires and added an unusual flavor to their
food. Nevertheless, the pioneers were grateful for this
unusual fuel source. Game for hunting often was scarce
and the basic food supplies they carried became
monotonous. Helen Carpenter wrote, "...one does like a
change and about the only change we have from bread
and bacon, is bacon and bread."

Emigrant Rev. Samuel Parker reported:

*Dry bread and bacon consisted our breakfast, dinner
and supper. The bacon we cooked when we could
obtain wood for fire; but when nothing but green grass
could be seen, we ate our bacon without cooking.*

With an entry recording more severe conditions, Clark
Thompson in 1850 wrote, "Looked starvation in the face.
I have seen men on passing an animal that has starved to
death on the plains, stop and cut out a steak, roast and
eat it and call it delicious."

Travel was immensely challenging. Henry Allyn in
1852 wrote, "We have good roads comparatively. We
mean good roads if the sloughs are not belly deep and
the hills not right straight up and down and not rock
enough to turn the wagon over."

Amelia Hadley in 1851 recorded another hazard on
the roadway, "There is some of the largest rattle snakes in
this region I ever saw, being from 8 to 12 ft. long, and
about as large as a man's leg about the knee. This is no
fiction at all."

Their daily discomforts are hard to comprehend.
Margaret A. Frink in 1850 wrote:

*The road to-day was very hilly and rough. At night
we encamped within one mile of Fort Hall.
Mosquitoes were as thick as flakes in a snow-storm.
The poor horses whinnied all night, from their bites,
and in the morning the blood was streaming down
their sides.*

Despite their struggles, their journal often recorded their optimism. Amelia Stewart Knight in 1853 wrote,

Raining all day...and the boys are all soaking wet and look sad and comfortless. The little ones and myself are shut up in the wagons from the rain. Still it will find its way in and many things are wet; and take us all together we are a poor looking set, and all this for Oregon...I am thinking as I write, "Oh Oregon, you must be a wonderful country."

To lift their weary spirits, the travelers often took solace and joy in music. Catherine Sager wrote, "There were several musical instruments in the company; and these sounded out clear and sweet on the evening air while gay talk and merry laughter went on around the camp fire."

Amelia Hadley in 1851 recorded, "We are a merry crowd. While I journalize, John of the company is playing the violin, which sounds delightful way out here. My accordion is also good as I carry it in the carriage and play as we travel."

Benjamin Cleavor wrote in 1848, "The evening meal is just over. Near the river a violin makes lively music, and some youths improvise a dance; in another quarter a flute whispers its lament to the deepening night."

Moving west across today's Wyoming, the pioneers reached a spot called the "Parting of the Ways" where the trail split. Many wagon trains divided there with some veering left toward California while others followed the right fork on to Oregon. Sometimes even large family groups would separate to diversify their risk. The spot was the sight of many tearful farewells. Wagon ruts eroded by the dividing wagons are still visible today.

Those traveling toward Oregon made their way to Fort Bridger, built by famous mountain man Jim Bridger in 1843 to supply the travelers. Ever the opportunist, Bridger wrote, "I have established a small fort with blacksmith shop and iron in the road of the emigrants...by the time they get there, [they] are in want of all kinds of supplies."

Although many pioneers expressed fear of the Native Americans, there was little violence recorded along the trail. Travelers traded with the natives and they served as guides. John Minto in 1844 wrote, "To complete our satisfaction a cavalcade of Indian women now came along with horses loaded with Camas roots. We purchased some fresh roots to boil with our game...We bought all the women had, fishhooks being our money."

Martha Gay Masterson recorded:

One pleasant evening some Indian boys wanted to display their skill with bow and arrow. When we gave them a biscuit, they would set it up, step off some distance and pierce it with an arrow. Father got a pan of biscuits and he would measure off a distance, set up one and tell them to shoot at it. The one who struck it first got it for his own. They had considerable sport over the biscuits.

John Burch McClane in 1843 wrote, "We arrived at Grande Rond. We had a feast from the Cayuse Indians. We had some nice elk meat and boiled it with dried huckleberries and plenty of flour. We had a royal meal..."

That same year, Ninevah Ford recorded:

At Fort Hall General McCarver started out ahead of the train towards the Salmon Falls with a few packers, and on approaching them discovered some Indians and he saw a red flag hoisted. He formed his men for battle. They marched up towards the Indians believing they meant to fight. When he got near enough he discovered that the red flag was a salmon split open and spread out as a sign to the packers that they had salmon for sale. So they marched up and bought some salmon.

The pioneer journey was so physically exhausting. The wagons carried the supplies and smaller children. Most pioneers walked the 2,000 miles as the wagons were primarily for supplies. Amelia Stewart Knight wrote in 1853, "We are creeping along slowly, one wagon after another, the same old gait, the same thing over, out of one mud hole into another all day."

Benjamin Cleavor in 1848 recorded the effect of the exhaustion, "...a drowsiness has fallen apparently on man and beast; teamsters fall asleep on their perches and even when walking by their teams."

Elizabeth Dixon Smith wrote in 1847:

*...my children give out with cold and fatigue and
could not travel and the boys had to unhitch the oxen
and bring them and carry the children on to
camp...We started this morning at sunrise and did
not get to camp until after dark and there was not
one dry thread on one of us, not even my babe, and I
was so fatigued that I could scarcely speak or step.*

The desperate fatigue left them more susceptible to
immune system breakdown, illnesses, and accidents.
Absolom Harden in 1847 recorded this heartbreaking
entry, "Mr. Harvey's young little boy Richard, 8-years-
old, went to get in the wagon and fell. The wheels run
over him and...he never moved."

Perhaps the pioneers' most terrifying fear was the
deadly sickness of cholera that claimed thousands of lives
along the trail. Jane D. Kellogg noted the rampant, deadly
disease in 1852:

*There was an epidemic of cholera, think it was caused
from drinking water from the holes dug by campers.
All along was a graveyard most any time of day you
could see people burying their dead. Some places five
or six graves in a row...*

Harriet Scott was 11 years old when she made the
journey with her family in 1852. Along the way, her
mother and younger brother both became ill and died.
Harriet wrote, "When we came to Fort Walla Walla, we
saw a crowing rooster on a rail fence. Oh, how we cried.

There we stood, a travel-worn, weary-heart, and home-sick group crying over a rooster crowing."

John Clark wrote:

One woman and two men lay dead on the grass and some more ready to die. Women and children crying, some hunting medicine and none to be found. With heartfelt sorrow, we looked around for some time until I felt unwell myself. Got up and moved forward one mile, so as to be out of hearing of crying and suffering.

Esther McMillan Hanna wrote

Passed six fresh graves!... Oh, 'tis a hard thing to die far from friends and home—to be buried in a hastily dug grave without shroud or coffin—the clods filled in and then deserted, perhaps to be food for wolves...

Jane Gould wrote

On the afternoon we passed a lonely nameless grave on the prairie. It had a headboard. It called up a sad train of thoughts. To my mind it seems so sad to think of being buried and left alone in so wild a country with no one to plant a flower or shed a tear over one's grave.

The non-profit Oregon-California Trails Association estimates that approximately one of every 10 people along the trail died. Over a span of 25 years through the middle of the 1800s, the number of deaths along the trail may have been as many as 65,000 along the entire 2,000 miles, or an average of up to 30 graves per mile.

Certainly, the exhaustion, sickness, and hardships led to frustrations and doubts. Lucy Ide was clearly troubled when she wrote, "Well, well, this is not so romantic; thoughts will stray back (in spite of all our attempts to the contrary) to the comfortable homes we left and the question – is this a good move? – but echo answers not a word."

Keturah Belknap wrote,

> ...in the next wagon behind ours a man and woman are quarreling. She wants to turn back and he won't go so she says she will go and leave him with the children and he will have a good time with that crying baby...

Lavina Porter could barely contain her despair when she wrote:

> I would make a brave effort to be cheerful and patient until the camp work was done. Then starting out...when I thought I had gone beyond hearing distance, I would throw myself down on the unfriendly desert and give way like a child to sobs and tears, wishing myself back home with my friends and chiding myself for consenting to take this wild goose chase.

TOWARD OREGON CITY

Continuing west into today's Idaho, the travelers
headed for Fort Hall, which had been established along
the Snake River in 1832 as a fur-trading post by United
States entrepreneur Nathaniel Wyeth. The British
Hudson's Bay Company purchased the fort in 1837. At
Fort Hall, travelers in need received assistance and a
much-appreciated taste of civilization.

Along this area, the trail paralleled the Snake River. At
the Three-Island Crossing, pioneers faced a difficult
choice. If they were willing to make a series of dangerous
river crossings, they would get a direct route to Fort
Boise. Others chose the safer route of continuing to follow
the Snake River south along a long bend, adding miles to
the journey.

Osborne Cross in 1849 wrote,

*After passing this morning through the valley in
which we encamped last evening, the road brought
us to the top of a high ridge, giving us a beautiful
view of the mountains, running east and west, and
parallel to the ridge over which we were passing. The
sight was very fine, as these mountains were the first
we had seen covered with pine since leaving Soda
springs. This range is high and rugged, with its base*

well wooded; those to the left were equally as much
so, while the Blue mountains to the northwest reared
their peaks in dark blue masses high above the rest,
and are covered with a growth of as beautiful timber
as can be found between here and the Pacific Ocean.

The trail soon ascended toward the lovely, but
formidable Blue Mountains of eastern Oregon and
Washington. The 1843 settlers cut a road over these
mountains to make them passable for the first time for
wagons. John Minto remembered the scene in 1844,

The sight from this mountain top is one to be
remembered while life lasts...Looking across this
grand valley westward the dark blue line of the
Cascade Range of Mountains appears a forest-clad
and impassable wall, out of which arise two immense
white cones called, as I subsequently learned, Mount
Hood and Mount Adams.

The pioneers eventually traveled down out of the Blue
Mountains and toward the Columbia River. John Ball
wrote, "It was a very interesting and gratifying sight to
look on the Columbia after our long and tedious
journey."
Esther G. McMillan Hanna in 1852 added,

Came out in an open prairie. The scenery is very
beautiful. Had a superb view of the Cascade
Mountains. To the west, Mount Hood, the loftiest of
these, was very visible and being covered with snow

*with the sun shining upon it, it looked like a golden
cloud in the distance, being 150 miles away! ... I
never enjoyed so rich a sight before!*

BY LAND OR RIVER

For thousands of years the Columbia River has
drained to the Pacific Ocean. Even as the Cascade
Mountains were being uplifted, the river eroded through.
But as the Oregon Trail pioneers approached the
Columbia River Gorge, no pathway remained along the
river shore. The steep bluffs of the Cascade Mountain
range rose directly beside the river's edge.

The river through this region was filled with rocks
from ages of landslides and floods, creating torrential
rapids. Parthenia Blank described the scene, "The banks
are precipitous and rocky, and several hundred feet high
in some places. Passed down to an immense pile of loose
rocks across the stream, over which the water runs with
great rapidity for six miles."

Reaching a dead-end, the pioneers had to build rafts
to float down the dangerous rapids. John C. Fremont in
1843 wrote,

*...the river forms the cascades in breaking over a
point of...masses of rocks...we again embarked, the
water being white with foam among ugly rocks, and
boiling into a thousand whirlpools. The boat passed
with great rapidity... through 2 miles of broken
water, we ran some wild-looking rapids.*

Jesse Applegate recorded this tragic tale in 1843:

...presently the boat began to rise and fall and rock from side to side...I began to think this was no ordinary rapid... when looking across the river I saw a smaller boat about opposite to us near the south bank... there was a wail of anguish, a shriek, and scene of confusion in our boat that no language can describe. The boat we were watching disappeared and we saw the men and boys struggling in the water. Father and Uncle Jesse, seeing their children drowning, were seized with frenzy, and dropping their oars sprang up from their seats and were about to leap from the boat to make a desperate attempt to swim to them, when mother and Aunt Cynthia, in voices that were distinctly heard above the roar of the rushing waters, by commands and entreaties, brought them to a realization of our own perilous situation, and the madness of an attempt to reach the other side of the river by swimming.

Lindsay Applegate, reported,

My son, ten-years-old, my brother Jesse's son Edward, same age, were lost. It was a painful scene beyond description. We dared not go to their assistance without exposing the occupants of the other boat to certain destruction. The bodies of the drowned were never recovered.

Because of tragedies like that of the Applegate family, the final portion of the trail developed several route variations into the Willamette Valley. The most popular was the Barlow Road. In October 1845, Samuel Barlow led a small party with 13 wagons from The Dalles on a southwest loop around the slopes of Mt. Hood. The next year the Oregon Provisional Legislature authorized Barlow to develop his trail into a toll road authorized to charge $5 per wagon and 10 cents per head of livestock. Forty men carved out an 80-miles trail to the Willamette valley. By the mid-1850's many emigrants bypassed the Columbia Gorge and chose instead to struggle along the mountain crossing. The pathway was rough and steep. Wagon wheels were damaged and axles broke. In some places, travelers had to loop ropes around trees, then – using the tree like a pulley – lower the wagons down steep hillsides, often with disastrous results. But the Barlow Road still was safer than floating goods, wagons and loved ones down the dangerous Columbia River.

FORT VANCOUVER

Downstream of the Cascade Rapids, along the north bank of the Columbia River and opposite of the site where the north-flowing Willamette River empties into the Columbia, the Hudson's Bay Company established their headquarters and dominated the development of the region for three decades.

John Ball described the area:

...we arrived at Fort Vancouver, which is on the north side of the river... It was quite an extensive stockade enclosure, on a prairie, some little back from the river, with the store houses, the houses for the Governor and gentlemen (as partners and clerks were called), and quite a garden; and for the servants – the Canadian Frenchmen – little houses outside the fort. This was the main station of the Hudson Bay Company west of the mountains. And to this place came up their shipping...100 miles up the river.

OREGON CITY

By way of the river or through the mountains, the fortunate finally reached their destination in the Willamette River Valley at a town called Oregon City. Overton Johnson described the new town:

There were three small churches, three stores, two blacksmiths shops, two flour mills and one weekly newspaper, the Oregon Spectator. My father purchased a house and lot and we moved into it soon after we arrived and commenced the sale of our boots and shoes.

John Ball wrote,

To be sure, the Willamette valley is a fine country, being a valley watered by a stream of that name, fifty miles wide and say one hundred and fifty long with a coast range on the west and towering Cascade range on the east, crowned by Mount Hood, in the bright summer days ever in sight.

Henry Garrison wrote of relief and reality,

Our journey is ended, our toils are over, but I have not tried to portray the terrible conditions we were placed in. No tongue can tell, nor pen describe the heart rending scenes through which we passed.

Loren Hastings understood the journey's completion could be a blend of joy and sadness as he wrote, "I look back upon the long, dangerous and precarious emigrant road with a degree of romance and pleasure; but to others it is the graveyard of their friends."

James Miller celebrated with this entry:

We were happy, after a long and tedious tour, to witness the home of civilization. To see mills, storehouses, shops. To hear the noise of the workman's hammer; to enjoy the warm welcome of countrymen and friends.

Rebecca Ketcham in 1853 described the Oregon Trail this way, "I am very surprised to find such a well-beaten road as broad as 8 or 10 common roads in the States, and with a very little work could be made one of the most beautiful roads in the world."

Father Pierre-Jean DeSmet in 1851 recorded "These intrepid pioneers of civilization have formed the broadest, longest and most beautiful road in the whole world - from the United States to the Pacific Ocean."

IMPACT

In 1818, the United States and Great Britain agreed to equal access for traders in the Northwest. The two countries extended their shared claim to the area for the next 28 years. But due to the enormous influx of American settlers that emigrated to the Northwest along the Oregon Trail, Britain in 1846 released their claim below the 49th parallel of latitude, which still serves as the United States and Canadian border.

Migration to the west coast was greatly boosted in 1849 as a result of the California Gold Rush. In 1850, as Congress passed the Oregon Donation Land Act which offered an astounding 640 free acres to any couple who would stake and develop their claim.

In 1853, a portion of the territory north of the Columbia River was organized into the Washington Territory. Most of the population had settled to the south of the Columbia River and Oregon joined the federal union in 1859 as the thirty-third state.

Travel along the Oregon Trail declined after 1855 when the Panama Railroad was completed across the Isthmus of Panama and connected United States steamships more easily to the west coast. Pioneers continued traveling the trail during the Civil War.

Transportation dramatically changed again in 1869 when the first transcontinental railroad was completed.

The great westward migration ushered Washington to statehood in 1889 and Idaho the following year in 1890. Oregon's population had grown to more than 300,000.

Pioneer Catherine Sager summarized the growth of the region:

> *Surely if the way of the pioneer is hard and beset with dangers, at least the long years bring at last the realization that life, patiently and hopefully lived, brings its own sense of having been part... of the onward move to better things – not for self alone, but for others.*

Hope for a better future was the primary motivation of the Oregon Trail pioneers. Hope for a new life, work, home, family, and more. They made the journey in search of opportunity. More than 300,000 migrated to the Oregon Territory to fulfill their dreams of a new life in a land of abundant possibilities. Examples like Harriet Scott, who made the Oregon Trail journey with her family in 1852 when she was only 11 years old. She endured many hardships along the trail but lived a long life, passing away in Washington state 78 years later in 1930 at age 89.

But the story of James Addison Bushnell provides one of the most dramatic illustrations of the appeal and ultimate benefits of traveling to Oregon.

In the spring of 1852, James Addison Bushnell journeyed to Oregon. He left his young wife and son in Missouri while he went ahead to lay a foundation for their new life.

In the autumn of 1852, hearing of the Gold Rush in California, Bushnell decided to try his luck in the gold fields, hoping to strike it rich. Amazingly, he had some success and wrote to his wife and mother to set out on their journey to meet him in Oregon.

But mail service was uncertain and after months passed without a response, Bushnell grew concerned.

So, in July of 1853, he took his $400 savings and boarded a ship to Panama. No railroad or canal had been built at that time, so with mules and boats, he crossed the Isthmus to the Atlantic side. He caught a ship back to New York. He took a train to Chicago, a steamboat down the Illinois River and up the Mississippi and Missouri Rivers. By stagecoach and walking, he finally arrived back to his home in Missouri after a 15,000-mile-journey – only to learn that his family had departed westward three months earlier on the Oregon Trail.

So, Bushnell, made his return journey in reverse, back to New York, back to Panama, over the Isthmus, up to San Francisco, and back to Oregon City. He returned to the Willamette River valley financially broke.

He searched until November of 1853 when he finally was reunited with his family. They had been apart for 20 months and Bushnell had crossed the continent three times. Moving southward along the Willamette river to break away from the crowds of immigrants, the Bushnells settled near Eugene, Oregon.

In 1895, Bushnell was one of the founders of the Eugene Divinity School which is still in operation today as Northwest Christian College. He served as president of its board of regents until his death. His autobiography beautifully illustrates the rewards of having braved the Oregon Trail. He wrote:

> *Today is my eightieth birthday and still finds me on the shores of time... Some of the children had planned a surprise for me in the shape of gathering of the children and relatives and some of the old pioneers who were my friends and associates in earlier years... A table was set under the trees in the yard and loaded down with good things to eat to which about thirty sat down and enjoyed it to the fill...*

Four years later, Bushnell wrote:

> *Another year has gone to join the many past. All its joy - and I have had my share of them. All its sorrow - and it seems as if I had had more than my share of them, lie buried in the past. In the future lie the few months or years, I know not how few – God knows they can't be many, but I know I am in His care. I am nearly 84 and with loving children and kind friends, with all this world's goods and more than I can use. With good health the future stretches before like the going down of the sun on a summer's day.*

CLOSING

More than 300,000 pioneers like James Bushnell endured the journey west in search of opportunities for themselves and their families to create a brighter future. In so doing, they shaped the destiny of the Pacific Northwest and the United States.

My name is Bill Wiemuth and I thank you for joining me for this History Highlights book about the Oregon Trail pioneers. This is such an inspiring story. And the participants wrote so wonderfully about their experiences. It certainly has been my pleasure researching and sharing with you highlights of these incredible events.

I also hope you are developing an ever-growing fascination for history. At HistoryHighlights.com, explore our amazing collection of books, audiobooks, and 200+ video presentations offering you fascinating true stories in less than an hour.

There is so much to explore, learn, and enjoy. I know you will savor every moment. Please tell your friends and family about History Highlights. And connect with us online to enjoy FREE eBooks, audiobooks, and video programs! Learn more at HistoryHighlights.com.

We have spotlighted fascinating true stories such as the international intrigue and secret deals that enabled The Louisiana Purchase. A two-book set shares the tales of the Lewis and Clark Expedition. Another book illuminates the remarkable role of the Mississippi River. Or explore the impact on the Civil War of the Union's Anaconda Plan, intended to cripple the South's economy by controlling the Confederate coastline and waterways. The story of the first steamboat to travel down the Mississippi River is an adventure where everything that could go wrong did go wrong. But that riveting drama changed U.S. economy and history forever. Our Mark Twain and the Mississippi River presentation shares how the river impacted Twain's life, career, and writings.

America's history is filled with so many amazing stories to learn and explore. I know you will enjoy every moment of it. Thank you for sharing your time on this journey of discovery. Please recommend our HistoryHighlights.com books and learning programs to your friends and family. Review recent editions of our free monthly history newsletter and subscribe at HistoryHighlights.com.

PLEASE – A QUICK REVIEW.

Your review of this book is one of the primary ways we expand to find a new and growing audience of readers. Please leave your review in just few seconds at this link:

https://amzn.to/44vSwdv

Thank you so much!

We have many more books available to explore and enjoy in a variety of formats including eBooks, paperbacks, audiobooks. We also have a site offering more than 200 history video presentations. Please stay in touch with us with our free weekly HistoryHighlights.com newsletter. Enjoy free books, video presentations, and special insights. Preview samples and join our journey of discovery at HistoryHighlights.com

LEARN MORE

Following are just a few suggestions of resources to continue your exploration of the history and significance of the Oregon Trail. Enjoy your journey of discovery!

—BOOKS—

The Oregon Trail: An American Saga
by David Dary

The Oregon Trail
by Francis Parkman

The Oregon Trail: A New American Journey
by Rinker Buck

—VIDEOS—

The Oregon Trail
Steve Boettcher (Director)

Ken Burn's presents The West
Excellent PBS film.

—ONLINE—

Oregon-California Trails Association website:
https://www.octa-trails.org/

History Highlights Oregon Trail presentation:
https://gum.co/OrTrailvideo

History Channel website:
https://www.history.com/topics/westward-expansion/oregon-trail

A nice overview of Manifest Destiny:
https://www.history.com/topics/westward-expansion/manifest-destiny

National Park Service website:
https://www.nps.gov/oreg/learn/historyculture/index.htm

ABOUT THE AUTHOR

Bill Wiemuth

   I have loved every moment of my study and sharing
of history. In the last two decades, I have proudly
written, produced, and published a diverse collection of
books, audiobooks, and video presentations which
highlight amazing stories from United States history.

   As a speaker, I have presented these stories aboard
more than 500 cruises and delivered more than 3,000
presentations for cruise lines and organizations and
corporate events across the U.S. and internationally. I also
have appeared for numerous regional and national radio
television programs including National Public Radio,
CNN's *Headline News* and ABC's *Good Morning, America.*

My collection of 200+ video presentations has been published into its own online streaming video platform.

As a "reporter of the past," I value the skills I learned to earn a B.A. in Journalism from the University of Texas at Arlington. I also have earned an Alaska Naturalist certification from the University of Alaska - Southeast and I have been recognized as a Certified Interpretive Guide by the National Association of Interpretation which provides training for the National Park Service.

Learn more about me and my work to share stories from history, plus enjoy free books, audiobooks, video presentations, a weekly newsletter, and more. Visit us at HistoryHighlights.com.

Made in the USA
Middletown, DE
30 October 2023

41669398R00040